The Great Ukulele Hunt

by Kay Woodward
Illustrated by Emma Levey

OXFORD
UNIVERSITY PRESS

In this story ...

Pip and Kit run *Finders Squeakers* – a lost and found agency. They help return lost things to their owners.

· ·

island of Hawaii

Chapter 1
The holiday begins

"I love Hawaii!" cried Pip.

"How do you know?" asked Kit. "We haven't even landed the aeroplane yet."

"My guidebook says it's one of the most amazing places on earth!" replied Pip. She gazed out of the window at the island far below. "Take us down, Kit."

Pip gazed out of the window. Does this mean she had a quick look or that she looked for a long time? What might she see if she gazed down at the island?

It took Pip and Kit only seven minutes to find the beach.

"We are now officially on holiday," said Pip, hopping on to a deckchair. "For once, I plan to forget all about lost things and *relax*."

"Not me! I'm going to be very active!" cried Kit. Holding his surfboard in one paw, he splashed straight into the sea.

Kit wants to be active on this holiday. What is he going to do first? What other active things might he do?

Pip picked up her guidebook: *1001 Fun Facts about Hawaii*. She sighed happily.

"Yoo-hoo!" Kit called, from the top of a frothy wave. "Are you having a good time?"

Pip waved at him. "I am!" she shouted back. "How about you?"

"Awesome!" cried Kit, falling in.

"*Oh no!*" cried a voice. "It's gone!"

A girl with dark hair was zigzagging across the golden sand, peering under deckchairs.

"Where *is* it?" she wailed. "I won't be able to enter the competition without it!"

"What's going on?" said Kit, arriving back with dripping-wet fur.

"Sounds like someone needs our help!" Pip said urgently.

"Cheer up, Leilani!" said the girl's mother, who was close behind her. "It can't be far away."

Leilani sat down on the sand and began to sob. "The competition is t-t-tomorrow. I can't take p-p-part without m-m-my beautiful y-y-yellow—"

Pip and Kit waited anxiously for the next word.

"—UKULELE!" roared Leilani.

Chapter 2
The holiday ends

"What's a ukulele?" said Kit, under his breath.

"It's a small four-stringed guitar," replied Pip. "I read about them in my guidebook."

"Are you thinking what I'm thinking?" Kit asked.

Pip nodded. "The holiday is over. We have work to do!"

"Excellent!" said Kit, who didn't fancy falling off his surfboard again.

"I <u>intend</u> to find that missing ukulele," said Pip. She rubbed her chin thoughtfully. "Although, if the competition is tomorrow, we don't have long to solve the case."

"Tomorrow? Then there's not a moment to lose!" cried Kit. "The Great Ukulele Hunt is on!"

Pip <u>intends</u> to find the ukulele. This means she plans to find it. Can you think of something that you <u>intend</u> to do at the weekend?

Pip and Kit hunted under deckchairs. They searched by cafe tables. They even visited the ice-cream stand. Despite their best efforts, they couldn't find any sign of a ukulele. The only thing they found was a poster glued to a street lamp.

Pip and Kit can't find the ukulele despite putting in a lot of hard work. Can you think of a sentence that uses the word 'despite'? For example, you could say: *Despite the weather, I …*

"*Two* ukuleles have gone missing?" Kit said, scratching his head.

They saw another missing ukulele poster ... and then another.

That evening, as the sky faded from bright blue to candyfloss pink, Pip and Kit counted up all the posters they'd seen. Then they stared at each other in horror.

Seventy-five ukuleles were missing!

Chapter 3
The vanishing ukuleles

"The ukulele competition is tonight, and we still haven't found a single instrument," said Pip, the next morning. She scratched her head. "Where *are* they?"

"Actually, *there's* one," said Kit.

Pip stared goggle-eyed at a boy who was standing near a palm tree. He was strumming a blue ukulele.

"Let's get a bit closer!" suggested Pip.

They hurried along the beach, dodging an old, grey donkey and its owner, and skidded to a stop in a shower of sand.

"Oh, no!" said Kit.

The boy now had a garland of flowers hanging around his neck, but he was empty-handed.

"Where did my ukulele go?" he sobbed.

"HEE-HAW!"

Pip and Kit spun round to see the grey donkey standing nearby. Its face was framed with flowers.

"Let's interview that donkey," Pip said. "Maybe she saw something."

The donkey was called Melody.

"Why are you wearing all those garlands of flowers?" Kit asked.

"They're called *leis*," explained Melody. "I wear them because they ... er ... smell nice."

"*Two* ukuleles have gone missing?" Kit said, scratching his head.

They saw another missing ukulele poster ... and then another.

That evening, as the sky faded from bright blue to candyfloss pink, Pip and Kit counted up all the posters they'd seen. Then they stared at each other in horror.

Seventy-five ukuleles were missing!

Chapter 3
The vanishing ukuleles

"The ukulele competition is tonight, and we still haven't found a single instrument," said Pip, the next morning. She scratched her head. "Where *are* they?"

"Actually, *there's* one," said Kit.

Pip stared goggle-eyed at a boy who was standing near a palm tree. He was strumming a blue ukulele.

"Let's get a bit closer!" suggested Pip.

They hurried along the beach, dodging an old, grey donkey and its owner, and skidded to a stop in a shower of sand.

"Oh, no!" said Kit.

The boy now had a garland of flowers hanging around his neck, but he was empty-handed.

"Where did my ukulele go?" he sobbed.

"HEE-HAW!"

Pip and Kit spun round to see the grey donkey standing nearby. Its face was framed with flowers.

"Let's interview that donkey," Pip said. "Maybe she saw something."

The donkey was called Melody.

"Why are you wearing all those garlands of flowers?" Kit asked.

"They're called *leis*," explained Melody. "I wear them because they … er … smell nice."

"Have you seen any ukuleles?" Pip asked.

Melody gave a slight twitch.

Just then Melody's owner called out. He was an old man with silvery hair and a multi-coloured shirt. "Melody!" he said. "We'd better get home. It's time for your lunch."

"Um, sorry," said Melody to Pip. "Time to go!"

She trotted away.

Melody gave a slight twitch. Does this mean she shook a lot or a little bit? Why do you think she did this?

"Let's see if anyone else can help us," suggested Kit.

"Look! There's a Hawaiian goose," said Pip.

"We're looking for seventy-five ... sorry, seventy-*six* missing ukuleles," Kit explained to the goose, who was called Nina.

"Do you have any information that might help us to find them?" added Pip.

Nina scratched her head with her foot. "I can't tell you about the ukuleles," she said, "but I can tell you it's not the first time the competition has been under threat. Poor Bud Gaston …"

"What happened?" Pip asked.

"Oh, it was a long time ago," said Nina, shrugging. "Now I'm off to meet some friends, and I really must fly."

"That was useful," said Pip, writing in her notebook.

"Was it?" said Kit, uncertainly.

"Oh yes," said Pip. "We need to get to the library. Kit, can you get us there really fast?"

Kit grinned. He pulled his skateboard out from behind a palm tree and gave Pip a helmet. "Climb aboard and hold on really tight."

Chapter 4
At the library

In no time at all, they screeched to a halt in front of the library, which was a smart building with a high ceiling.

"Where can I look at old newspapers?" Pip asked a friendly gecko that was clinging to a wall.

The gecko unstuck one foot from the wall and gestured towards a large room. "In there," she said.

Kit began to flick through the yellowy newspapers with one paw. "What are we looking for anyway?" he asked.

"Anything about the previous ukulele competition that Nina mentioned," Pip replied.

Slowly, they made their way through the enormous pile of newspapers until …

"I've found it!" cried Kit.

The Hawaii Post

Bud's Ukulele Dream is Over

Bud Gaston was horrified to discover that his ukulele strings had been snipped by a rival at this year's Great Ukulele Competition. Bud was expected to win, but by the time he'd got some new strings the competition was over. "I'll be back!" promised Bud, with tears in his eyes. "Just wait and see!"

"We need to find Bud Gaston," said Pip. "I have a feeling that he'll know what's happened to the missing ukuleles." She checked the date on the newspaper. "It won't be easy. This paper is over twenty years old!"

"It might be easier than you think," said Kit. He pointed to the photo of Bud. Beside him was a donkey. It was Melody.

"Melody's owner is Bud Gaston!" said Pip. "Kit, can you get us to the beach really, really fast?"

Kit put his helmet back on and gave a nod. "Climb aboard and hold on really, really tight!" he said.

They rocketed along the streets, and Kit performed a trick on every corner. He whooped each time he changed direction.

Pip missed it all. Her eyes were squeezed tightly shut.

Chapter 5
The Great Ukulele Competition

At the beach, people were beginning to gather for the competition, but nobody had a ukulele.

Pip and Kit couldn't see Melody or Bud Gaston anywhere, but they did see Nina. She waved a webbed foot at them. "Have you found the ukuleles?" she called.

"Not yet!" replied Pip.

"Maybe I can help," said Nina. "What you need is a bird's-eye view of the island."

"Wow," said Kit, clambering on to Nina's back. "This is what I call flying in style!"

They soared into the air, circling the island until they heard a faint strumming far below.

"Someone's playing a ukulele!" cried Nina. "We're going down!"

The music was soft and soothing. The sound floated out from the open window of a pretty blue-and-white cottage.

Kit sighed. "I've never heard anything so lovely," he said, as they landed on the lawn.

"I know this tune!" said Nina. "It's *Aloha Oe*. It's a traditional Hawaiian song."

Pip, Kit and Nina crept closer to the cottage and peered through the window. Inside, Bud Gaston was holding a wooden ukulele and gently strumming the strings.

"We are in the presence of a great musician," murmured Pip, "... and a great thief!"

The room was full of stolen ukuleles.

Pip, Kit and Nina were in the presence of Bud Gaston. Does that mean that they were close to him or that they were far away?

"What now?" whispered Kit.

"Now," said Pip calmly, "we need to get those ukuleles back to their owners." She turned to Nina. "Can you call some friends?"

"Of course!" Nina said, flapping off into the sky.

A short time later, she was back with a flock of Hawaiian geese.

Everything happened very quickly after that.

When Melody saw all the geese, she began to HEE-HAW very loudly. Bud Gaston rushed outside.

The flock of geese flew inside the cottage as soon as the door was opened. Each one picked up a ukulele. Then the birds soared away.

Bud knew that he'd been <u>defeated</u>.

Who helped Pip and Kit to <u>defeat</u> Bud and Melody? What did they do to stop him?

At the beach, Bud told his story to everyone.

"I'm sorry," said Bud, sadly. "Years ago, someone cheated, so I couldn't enter the competition. It had a big <u>influence</u> on my life. I thought that if I borrowed everyone else's ukuleles this year, I'd be the only competitor. Then I'd win."

The other ukulele players couldn't help feeling a bit sorry for Bud. They agreed to forgive him.

"Now we can *all* take part in the competition!" said Leilani.

Someone else cheating had a big <u>influence</u> on Bud. What <u>influence</u> do you think it had? How do you think Bud feels now?

"So how *did* Bud take the ukuleles?" asked Kit.

"He gave each of the ukulele players a lei," explained Pip. "Then, while they were putting on their flower garland, he took their ukulele."

"At least he's learned his lesson now," said Kit.

"Now, let's relax and watch the competition," said Pip happily.

"I can't." Kit grinned. "Melody is letting me borrow one of Bud's old ukuleles. I'm taking part!"

Read and discuss

Read and talk about the following questions.

Page 3: Pip gazed out of the window. What other words could you use instead of 'gazed'?

Page 4: Do you like to be active at the weekends? What sort of things to do you like to do?

Page 9: What does Kit intend to do at the end of the story?

Page 10: Can you explain something that Pip and Kit had to overcome to solve the mystery? You could say: *Despite the … Pip and Kit …*

Page 15: Can you give a slight nod of your head?

Page 27: Have you ever been in the presence of a musician? Who was it?

Page 29: Bud was defeated in the ukulele competition many years ago. What happened?

Page 30: Can you name someone who has a big influence on you?